ANIMAL HOMES

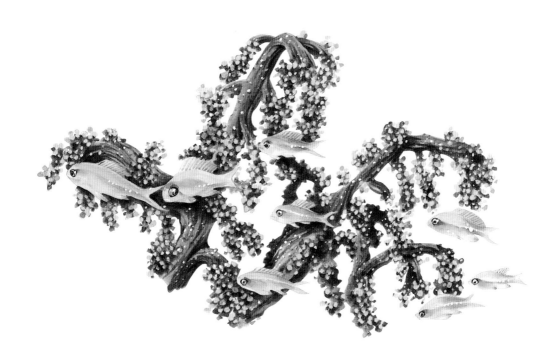

**McGraw-Hill
Children's Publishing**
A Division of The **McGraw·Hill** Companies

This edition published in the United States in 2002 by
Peter Bedrick Books, an imprint of
McGraw-Hill Children's Publishing,
A Division of The McGraw-Hill Companies
8787 Orion Place
Columbus, OH 43240

www.MHkids.com

ISBN 0-87226-689-3

Library of Congress Cataloging-in-Publication
Data is on file with the publisher.

Animal Homes created and produced by

MᶜRAE BOOKS

via de' Rustici, 5, Florence (Italy)
tel. +39 055 264 384
fax +39 055 212 573
e-mail: mcrae@tin.it

Project Manager: Anne McRae
Graphic Design: Marco Nardi
Illustrations: Antonella Pastorelli
Picture Research: Elzbieta Gontarska
Editing: Joanna Buck
Layout and cutouts: Adriano Nardi, Laura Ottina, Filippo Delle Monache

Color separations: Litocolor (Florence)
Printed and bound by Artegrafica, Verona, Italy

CORAL REEFS

Text by Anita Ganeri
Illustrations by Antonella Pastorelli

PETER BEDRICK BOOKS

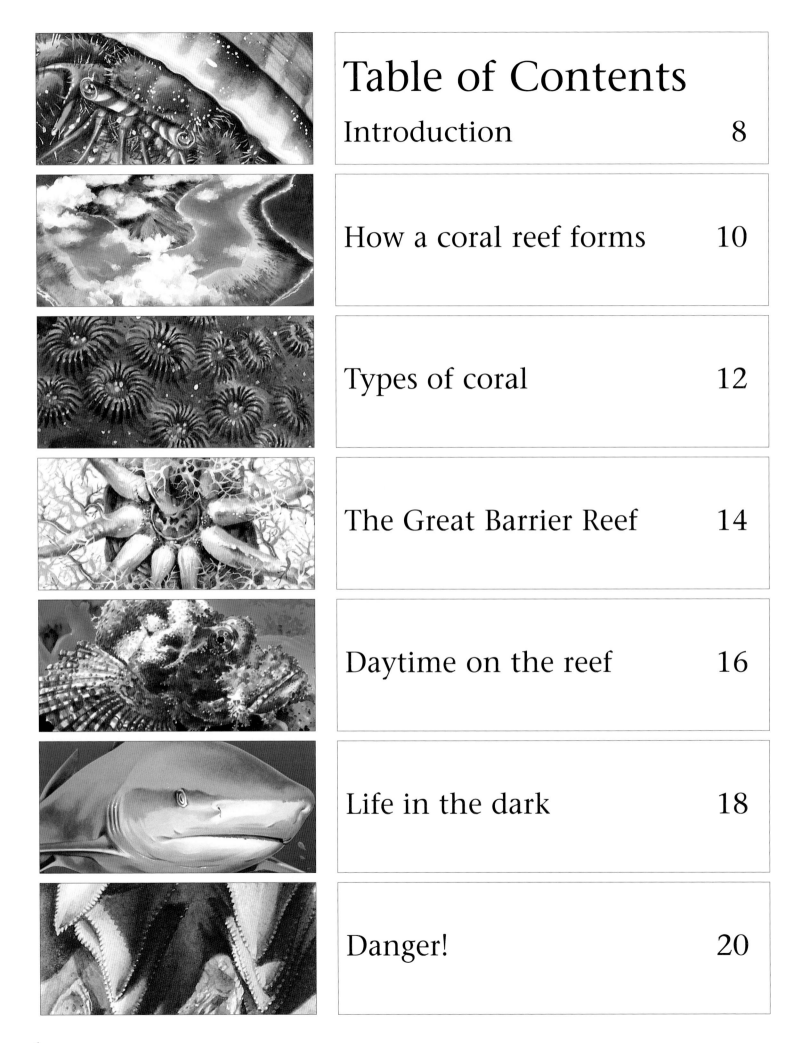

Table of Contents

Introduction

Coral reefs grow in tropical seas where the water is warm and shallow. Sometimes described as underwater rain forests, they are the richest habitats in the sea. From brightly striped sea snakes to giant clams, coral reefs are overflowing with life and color. Here you will find thousands of species of fish and coral, together with sea slugs, starfish, and anemones.

What is coral?

Scientists used to think that coral was a plant. However, today we know that coral reefs are made by small animals called polyps that are related to jellyfish and sea anemones. Coral polyps produce a hard, outer skeleton in the shape of a cup. It takes millions of them to form a coral reef.

Sea snails

Brilliantly colored sea snails, like the one shown below, live on the coral reef. Many sea snails graze on the algae growing on the rocks and coral. Others feed on coral animals, such as sea anemones.

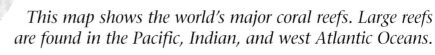

This map shows the world's major coral reefs. Large reefs are found in the Pacific, Indian, and west Atlantic Oceans.

Water conditions

Coral grows in partnership with tiny plants called algae. This means that coral reefs can only grow in warm, clean, shallow water where there is plenty of sunlight for the algae to photosynthesize (make food).

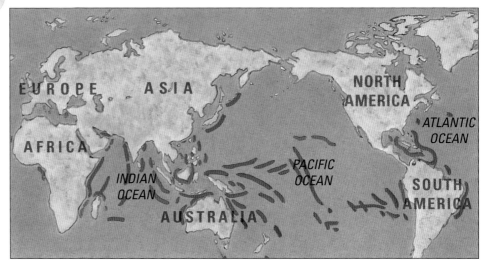

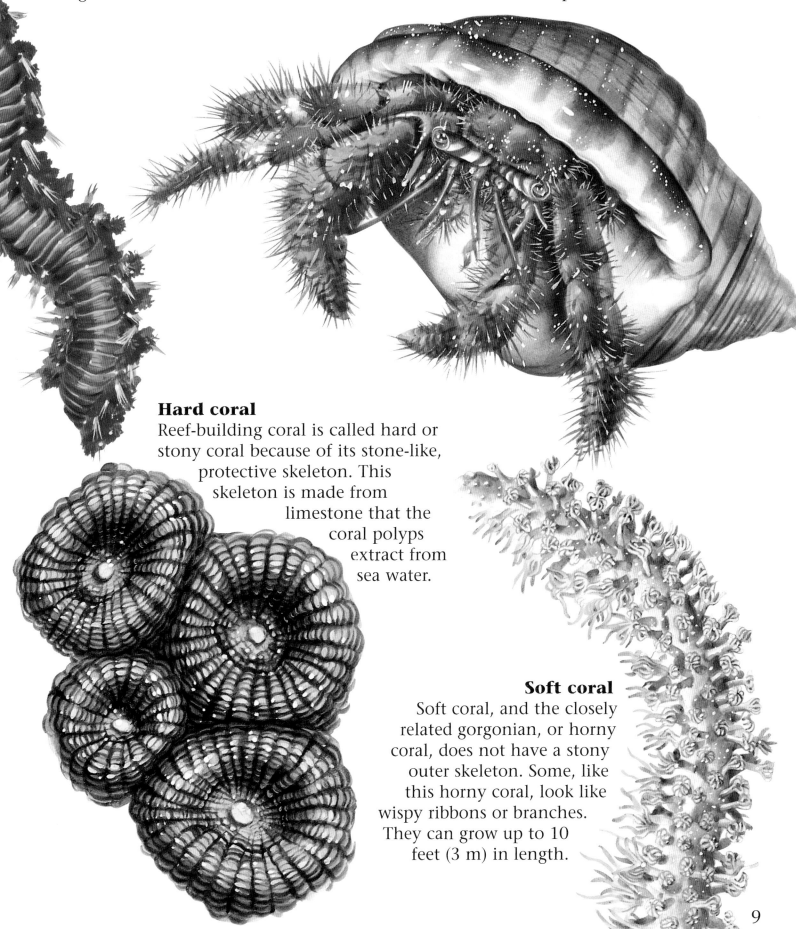

Sea worms
Hundreds of species of sea worms live in the sand or in coral burrows. Many are brightly colored. Some even glow in the dark.

Moving house
Hermit crabs can be found on the coral reef. Because they don't have shells of their own, hermit crabs borrow discarded sea shells to protect their soft bodies.

Hard coral
Reef-building coral is called hard or stony coral because of its stone-like, protective skeleton. This skeleton is made from limestone that the coral polyps extract from sea water.

Soft coral
Soft coral, and the closely related gorgonian, or horny coral, does not have a stony outer skeleton. Some, like this horny coral, look like wispy ribbons or branches. They can grow up to 10 feet (3 m) in length.

How a coral reef forms

Coral reefs have been on Earth for more than 450 million years. Reefs are built by huge colonies of hard, or stony coral. When the coral polyps die, their hard skeletons are left behind and build up the reef. Coral grows very slowly, at the rate of only a couple of inches (5 cm) a year. A colony the size of a soccer ball takes about 20 years to form.

Fringing reefs

A fringing reef (shown below) grows in shallow water along a coastline, forming a border along the shore. These reefs often grow on the slopes of volcanic islands.

Barrier reefs

Like a fringing reef, a barrier reef (shown above) grows along coastlines, but is separated from the shore by a stretch of water, such as a lagoon or a strait.

Coral atolls

The Pacific and Indian Oceans are dotted with thousands of tiny coral islands, called atolls (shown at left).

How a coral atoll begins

A coral atoll forms when a volcanic island rises from the sea (1). A reef grows around the island when it breaks the surface (2). As the island slowly sinks back into the sea, the coral keeps growing to form a round atoll around a deep lagoon (3).

1.

2.

3.

Coral polyps

Inside its hard skeleton, a coral polyp looks like a tiny sea anemone with a simple, tube-like body and a mouth lined with stinging tentacles.

Some polyps grow as buds on other polyps. They do not separate from their parents, so a colony builds up.

Inside a polyp

Tentacle

Pharynx (mouth)

Digestive cavity

The outer wall

Partition

Connective tissue

Reproduction

Not all coral reproduces by forming buds. Some release eggs into the water. Tiny larvae hatch and drift in the water until they find a rock or part of the reef to affix themselves to. Then they start to grow their stony, cup-shaped skeletons.

How coral feeds

Coral polyps use their stinging tentacles to catch passing water creatures. Most coral feed only at night. By day, it hides its tentacles away in its limestone cup. The tiny algae that grow inside coral polyps also provide the coral with food.

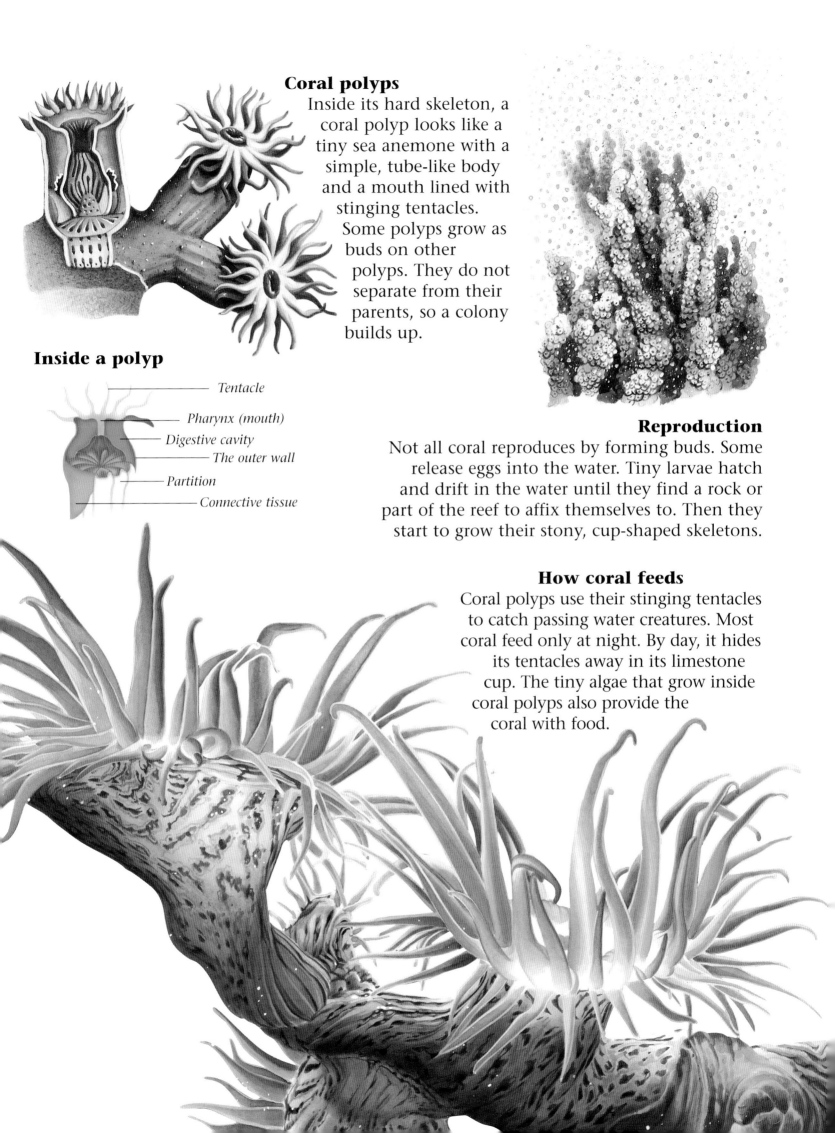

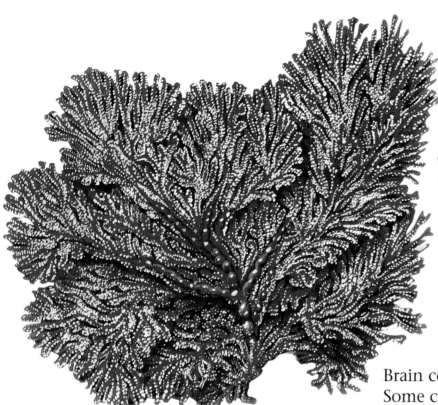

Gorgonian coral

The brightly colored gorgonian coral, shown to the left, has a flexible, horny skeleton rather than a stony case. Gorgonian coral often grows in bushy clumps or fan shapes under ledges or on cave roofs in the coral reef.

Brain coral

Brain coral gets its name because it looks so much like a human brain. Its polyps grow in long ridges, like waves. Brain corals are stony corals. Some can grow to more than 6 feet across (about 2 m).

Types of coral

Among the layers of reef-builders one can find coral shaped like large mushrooms, branching antlers, delicate feathers, and miniature trees. Up to 150 different coral types may be found on one reef. Living coral is brightly colored, in shades of pink, blue, purple, yellow, and green. But the color is only skin-deep. The dead coral below is chalky white.

Stony coral

There are about 1,000 different species of stony coral in the world. Living stony coral is usually a yellow, brown, or olive color, depending on the color of the algae that lives on it.

Soft coral

Many species of soft coral live on the reef, although they do not help to build it. Some are bright orange, pink, or yellow. Others are dull and leathery. Some soft coral moves around the reef, drifting on the ocean's currents.

Lights and colors

Many kinds of coral look drab and dull, overgrown with algae and hidden by sand. But if an ultraviolet light is shone on them, they burst into an array of light and color. No one knows why coral starts to glow. It might be because it helps the algae that grows inside it to photosynthesize.

Twice the size

The meat polyp, or button coral, is usually found in deep or shaded areas on the reef. During the day, it grows to almost twice its size. It feeds at night by extending its ring of tentacles to trap sea creatures.

Fire coral

The fire coral's bright yellow coloring makes it easy to spot. Its tentacles are packed with poison, and they deliver a painful, burning sting to any fish or human that brushes past.

Organ pipe coral

The stony tubes of this unusual coral look like tiny organ pipes. The pipes are built by large, feathery polyps that fan out to collect particles of food. After feeding, the polyps withdraw into their pipes.

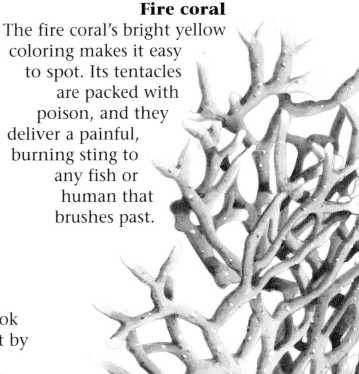

Moorish idol
The long snout, bold stripes, and pointed, sweeping fins make the Moorish idol an unforgettable sight. This fish was once sacred to Muslims.

Cleaner fish
Small fish, called wrasse, run a cleaning service on the coral reef. Large fish, quite capable of eating the wrasse, stay still while the wrasse pick dead skin and parasites off of them. The fish even allow the wrasse inside their mouths to clean leftover food from their sharp teeth!

Sea cucumbers
Sea cucumbers are small, sausage-shaped creatures, related to starfish and sea urchins. They have a ring of tentacles around their mouths for catching tiny particles of food from the sand as they crawl along the sea bed.

Warning colors
A sea slug's bright colors are a warning to predators. Many species are poisonous and taste terrible. Sea slugs crawl over the coral or along the sea bed. Some feed on coral. Others eat sea sponges, sea squirts, and sea anemones.

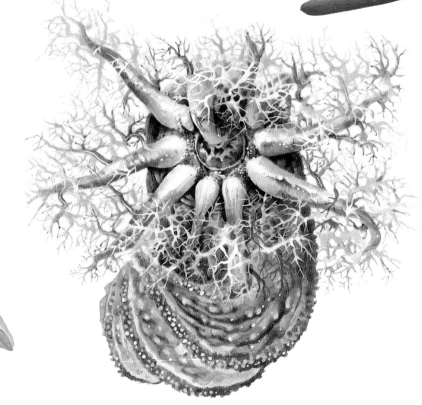

The Great Barrier Reef

Australia's Great Barrier Reef is the largest coral reef in the world and the biggest structure ever built by living organisms. It is home to an astonishing variety of animals, including at least 400 different species of coral and 1,500 species of fish. All of this makes it a rich feeding ground for predators, such as prowling reef sharks.

Reef sharks
Reef sharks spend about 4 to 6 hours each day feeding.

The Great Barrier Reef
The Great Barrier Reef stretches for 1,250 miles (2,016 km) along the northeast coast of Australia. It covers an area the size of England and Scotland combined, and is made up of about 3,000 individual reefs.

Triton conch
The triton conch drags its heavy shell behind it as it attacks a crown-of-thorns starfish. It cuts the starfish open, then sucks out its insides. The starfish feed on coral and have already destroyed large chunks of the Great Barrier Reef.

Stinging coral
The fish below has blundered into the tentacles of a tube coral. Rings of feathery tentacles surround the coral's mouth. They are dotted with tiny, stinging cells that are used to paralyze prey before it is digested.

Daytime on the reef

A coral reef is a crowded place. To avoid competition for food and space, life on the reef is carefully balanced between night and day. At daybreak, the reef bursts into color and life. Large numbers of fish leave their hiding places and start their search for food. Meanwhile, nocturnal fish, such as the scorpion fish, return to their shelters to rest.

Hawkfish perch
Most fish have a gas-filled swim bladder that keeps their bodies afloat in the water. But the hawkfish has to prop itself in a fork of coral to stop it from sinking. Most hawkfish hunt for tiny creatures on the sea floor.

Moontailed bullseyes
This group of bright red fish with half-moon tails rest after a busy night. Their extra-large eyes are designed to help them see at night, when they hunt for large plankton, crustaceans, and small fish.

Flying gurnard
Flying gurnards are sturdily built fish which usually live on the sea bottom. Their side fins are large and fan-like, and may be used to scare off predators. These fish can also leap out of the water and glide a short way through the air.

Loggerhead turtle
Loggerhead turtles cruise the reef, feeding on fish and mollusks. They can stay underwater for hours on end but need to surface regularly for air. At breeding time, female turtles leave the reef and lay their eggs on the sandy beaches of a coral island.

Clownfish
These black and yellow clownfish hide among the tentacles of a sea anenome.

Bearded scorpion fish
The bearded scorpion fish (above) finds a place to rest on the coral reef. It gets its name from the extra flaps of skin on its chin. Scorpion fish can change color to blend in with their surroundings.

17

Life in the dark

At night, the coral reef is transformed. Daytime creatures settle down to sleep in caves or holes in the coral. Then it is the reef's nocturnal residents' turn to come out and look for food. Among them are coral. They unfurl their tentacles to feed on tiny creatures, called plankton. Also on the prowl are hungry gray sharks, the most feared night hunters.

Cardinals under cover

As night falls, swarms of tiny cardinal fish pour out of their coral caves and spread out to feed under the cover of darkness. Their silvery color helps to hide them from hungry enemies, such as scorpion fish.

Nighttime nautilus

The nautilus shown at left has a shell divided into chambers. By regulating the amount of gas and fluid in it, the nautilus can make itself float, sink, or swim.

Fairy feast

By day, huge numbers of brilliantly colored fairy basslet fish hover above the reef, feeding on day-swimming plankton. At night, the whole school moves off to hide among the fronds, or leaf-like stems, of coral. Their half-moon shaped tails and bullet-shaped bodies help them to move quickly when in danger.

Night and day colors
At night, the fusilier fish sleeps on the sea bed. In the moonlight, its bright red color appears murky gray to help camouflage it. When it wakes up, the fish's red color returns, making it hard to see in the sunlit water.

Feather feeders
Feather stars, or crinoids, look like exotic plants, but these delicate animals are related to starfish. By day, they hide among the coral. At night, they anchor themselves on rocks and fan out their feathery arms to strain plankton from the water.

Puffer fish
These globular-shaped fish inflate themselves with air or water to protect themselves when they are disturbed. Their skin is usually prickly and tough, and many species are poisonous.

Danger!

Danger lurks around every corner on the coral reef, as hungry predators search for food. Some reef creatures are armed with poisonous prickles and spines. Others have razor-sharp teeth or venomous stingers. These fearsome features are also useful for scaring away would-be attackers.

Poisonous sea snakes

All 50 species of sea snakes use poison to kill their prey of fish and eels. Their poison is deadlier than a cobra's – just one drop could kill three people! However, sea snakes are normally quite shy and gentle, unless they are provoked.

Stinging jellyfish

The jellyfish's transparent body makes it difficult to see. In the water, it is a deadly hunter, armed with lethal stinging tentacles. It uses these to catch its prey of fish and to protect itself from harm.

Prickly characters

The strange-looking crown-of-thorns starfish can grow up to twenty arms from its body and is covered with thick spines. These creatures kill huge patches of coral by eating the soft-bodied polyps.

Coral trout attack

Coral trout are common on the reef. They swim slowly over the coral, looking harmless as they drift among the other fish. But if a fish dares to come too close, the trout suddenly pounces. Quick as a flash, it lunges and sucks the fish into its large mouth.

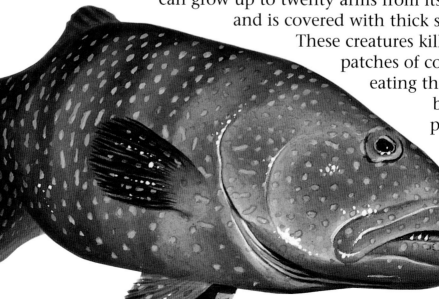

Scorpion fish disguise

At night, the scorpion fish comes out to hunt for tasty shrimp and fish. Its body is covered in different colored flaps of skin so that when it lies still on the sea bed, it looks just like a weed-covered rock. Then, when a shrimp swims past, the unseen scorpion fish strikes.

Shark attack

Sharks, the fiercest predators in the sea, visit the coral reef to enjoy the rich pickings. Their rows of razor-sharp teeth are lethal weapons for catching and killing prey. If one row of teeth wears out, another one slides forward to take its place.

Sharks use only the first two rows of teeth to tear their prey to pieces.

Surgeon fish

The surgeon fish gets its name from the two sharp, spike-like spines on either side of its tail. These spines normally lie flat in a groove in its skin. But if the fish is attacked, its spines stick upright and it swipes its tail from side to side, lashing out at its enemy.

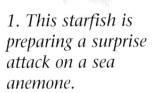

1. This starfish is preparing a surprise attack on a sea anemone.

2. The starfish attemps to wrap its long arms around its prey, ready to push out its stomach.

How a starfish eats

Starfish dine on coral, shellfish, and sea anemones. To eat a sea anemone, a starfish squeezes its stomach out of its body and smothers the anemone. It takes several hours to digest the anemone's flesh. Then the starfish pulls its stomach back in.

3. But the anemone is strong and frees itself from the arms of the starfish.

4. The anemone then pushes itself away from its predator.

Avoiding predators

For many coral reef creatures, each day is a battle to survive. Many of these animals have developed special features and skills for scaring off their predators and for staying alive. Some hide away or blend in with their background. Others use colors to confuse their enemies or poisons to protect themselves.

Sandy burrow
Underneath the coral reef, on the sea floor, lives the beautiful sea snail. If attacked, it burrows into the sand and waits until the danger is gone.

Poison protection
If a predator tries to attack a lionfish, it is in for a painful surprise. The lionfish's feathery fins are covered in poisonous spines that it jabs at its enemies.

Hidden in the sand
The crocodile fish buries itself in the sand for protection against predators or to hide itself from unsuspecting prey. Its color helps to camouflage it.

Anemone clownfish
Sea anemones have poisonous tentacles that kill small fish to feed. Strangely, clownfish live unharmed among the anemone's tentacles, where they are safe from predators. Their bodies are covered in a slimy mucus that stops them from being stung.

Time to flee

The flat, disc-like body of the angelfish, its long fins, and its vertical bands of color, give it an impressive appearance. Its body is designed to help it move quickly and easily through the water to avoid predators. The fish's coloring helps it to blend in with its surroundings.

False eyes

The butterfly fish has false eye spots near its tail and a dark stripe that hides its real eyes. These markings trick its enemies into attacking the wrong end of its body, giving the fish a chance to escape.

Crab hideaways

By day, many crabs hide away in nooks and crannies in the coral or in burrows in the sandy sea floor. Some cover themselves with tiny sponges or sea anemones for extra protection.

Porcupine fish

A porcupine fish's spines usually lie flat against its body. But if danger threatens, the fish gulps in water and blows itself up like a balloon. Its spines stick up like a porcupine's, scaring off predators.

Blending in

Some fish blend in so well with their surroundings that they are almost impossible for predators to spot. This fish's bright colors and cross-hatched markings allow it to hide among the coral stems.

Staying close to home

These tiny fish hide away in nooks and crannies in the coral. Even when they venture out to feed, they stay close to home. Then, if they sense danger nearby, they can quickly dart back inside again.

Special animals

Coral reefs are home to some of the most fascinating and exotic creatures found anywhere in the world. The marine life ranges from enormous seashells and strangely shaped fish, to delicate jellyfish and slugs disguised as plants. Coral reefs present a dazzling display of shapes, sizes, and colors, creating an amazing underwater wonderland.

Jellyfish

The Portuguese man-of-war

Man-of-war
The Portuguese man-of-war has highly poisonous, stinging tentacles up to 100 feet (30.5 m) long, that are used for catching prey. This giant is made up of thousands of tiny, individual animals joined together.

Super-sized seashells
Giant clams are the largest seashells in the world. They can measure over 3 feet (1 m) across and weigh more than a quarter of a ton (250 kg). The greenish-blue coloring on their "lips" is created by tiny algae.

Sea horses
Despite its strange shape, a sea horse is a tiny fish. A poor swimmer, it hovers in the water, propelling itself along with its back fin. If the current is strong, it uses its tail to cling to a piece of seaweed or coral to avoid being swept away.

Sea slug garden
Sea slugs are among the most unusual animals that live on the coral reef. The floating garden sea slug (shown above) stores green plant cells in its body. The plant cells take in sunlight to make food for the sea slug to consume.

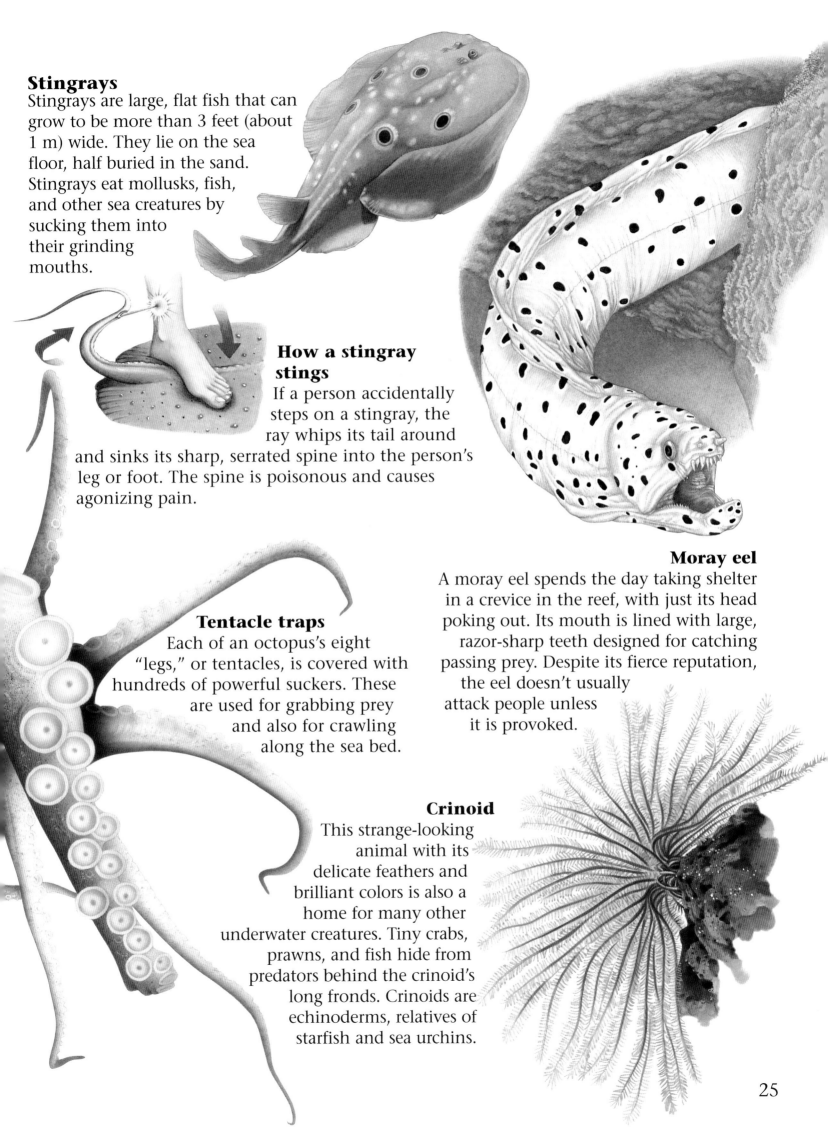

Stingrays

Stingrays are large, flat fish that can grow to be more than 3 feet (about 1 m) wide. They lie on the sea floor, half buried in the sand. Stingrays eat mollusks, fish, and other sea creatures by sucking them into their grinding mouths.

How a stingray stings

If a person accidentally steps on a stingray, the ray whips its tail around and sinks its sharp, serrated spine into the person's leg or foot. The spine is poisonous and causes agonizing pain.

Moray eel

A moray eel spends the day taking shelter in a crevice in the reef, with just its head poking out. Its mouth is lined with large, razor-sharp teeth designed for catching passing prey. Despite its fierce reputation, the eel doesn't usually attack people unless it is provoked.

Tentacle traps

Each of an octopus's eight "legs," or tentacles, is covered with hundreds of powerful suckers. These are used for grabbing prey and also for crawling along the sea bed.

Crinoid

This strange-looking animal with its delicate feathers and brilliant colors is also a home for many other underwater creatures. Tiny crabs, prawns, and fish hide from predators behind the crinoid's long fronds. Crinoids are echinoderms, relatives of starfish and sea urchins.

Coral reef fish

More species of fish make their homes on a coral reef than anywhere else in the sea. A small reef may have about 200 species. An amazing 2,000 species live on the Great Barrier Reef. Every shape and color of fish is found there, from vast schools of brilliant butterfly fish, hovering above the coral, to giant sharks and manta rays, prowling the edges of the reef.

Parrot fish
The parrot fish gets its name from its sharp, beak-like teeth. The beak is perfect for crunching away at the coral to get at the soft polyps and for scraping algae from the rocks.

Spiny hiding place
These shrimp fish are swimming head down in the coral, picking food from the sea bed. By day, they hover among a sea urchin's spines, perfectly camouflaged.

Triggerfish supper
Triggerfish have unusual feeding habits. Some feed on prickly, long-spined sea urchins. Others eat crown-of-thorns starfish. They flip the starfish over and start to eat them from underneath to avoid the longest spines.

Sweetlips
These spotted fish get their name from their large upper lips and rotruding jaws. They roam the reefs looking for algae and tiny crustaceans to eat.

Napoleon fish
Adult napoleon fish have thick lips and a large hump on their foreheads. They inhabit the outer reef slopes and lagoon reefs, and usually live alone or in pairs.

All change
On the outer slopes of the reef, schools of fairy basslets search for plankton to eat. These jewel-like fish are born as females, though some later turn into males. They live in mostly female groups, with just a few adult males.

27

From shore to shore

The trees and vegetation found on a coral island may have come from another island or place a long way away. Seeds are carried many miles by the wind, birds, or ocean currents. Coconut palm seeds have shells that can stay afloat in water for weeks, before being washed up on another island shore.

Island life

The rich vegetation and beautiful sandy beaches of tropical coral islands are home to some strange and wonderful animals. These islands are built on top of shallow coral reef platforms, which took thousands of years to form. Shrubs, grasses, palm trees, and mangroves cover their surfaces, creating some of the world's most spectacular scenery.

High-rise islands
The fringing coral reefs around a volcanic island may eventually end up as a coral island. This happens when parts of the reef rise above the water's surface after the volcano has subsided into the sea.

How do coral islands form?
Many coral islands start out as a series of shallow, interconnected lagoons. The action of the waves on the reef's edges breaks down the coral into sand and debris. This eventually fills the lagoons and forms several small islands, known as cays.

Extra-large sizes
The giant Aldabra tortoise is found on a small group of coral islands in the Indian Ocean. The species has evolved into its extra-large size because of the isolation of island life. It has been protected from predators and has little competition for the plant food it eats.

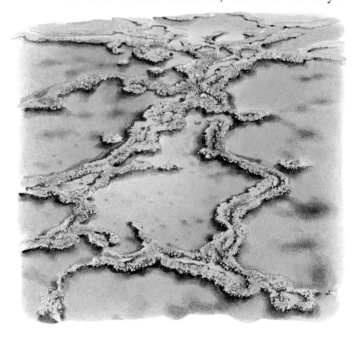

Clowning around
The booby bird gets its name from the Spanish word "bobo," which means clown. Early Spanish sailors called these birds bobos as they thought they were stupid. This was because the birds did not fly away when the sailors tried to hunt them.

Coral lagoons

The shallow, protected waters of coral lagoons attract a multitude of brightly colored fish. As the rising tide fills the lagoon, the fish swim in to explore the plants, coral, and sandy floors, in search of food. When the tide goes out, water pours out of the lagoon along with hundreds of fish, leaving parts of it empty except for the long, spindly roots of the mangroves.

Blackspot snapper
Blackspot snappers look for small fish and invertebrates (animals without backbones) to eat. They get their name from the large, round, black spot on their backs.

Mangroves
The exposed, arched roots of mangrove trees are a familiar sight in coral lagoons. Mangroves are the only trees that can grow in salt water. Their extensive system of roots helps to stop the erosion of coastal areas and provides protection and food for a number of marine organisms.

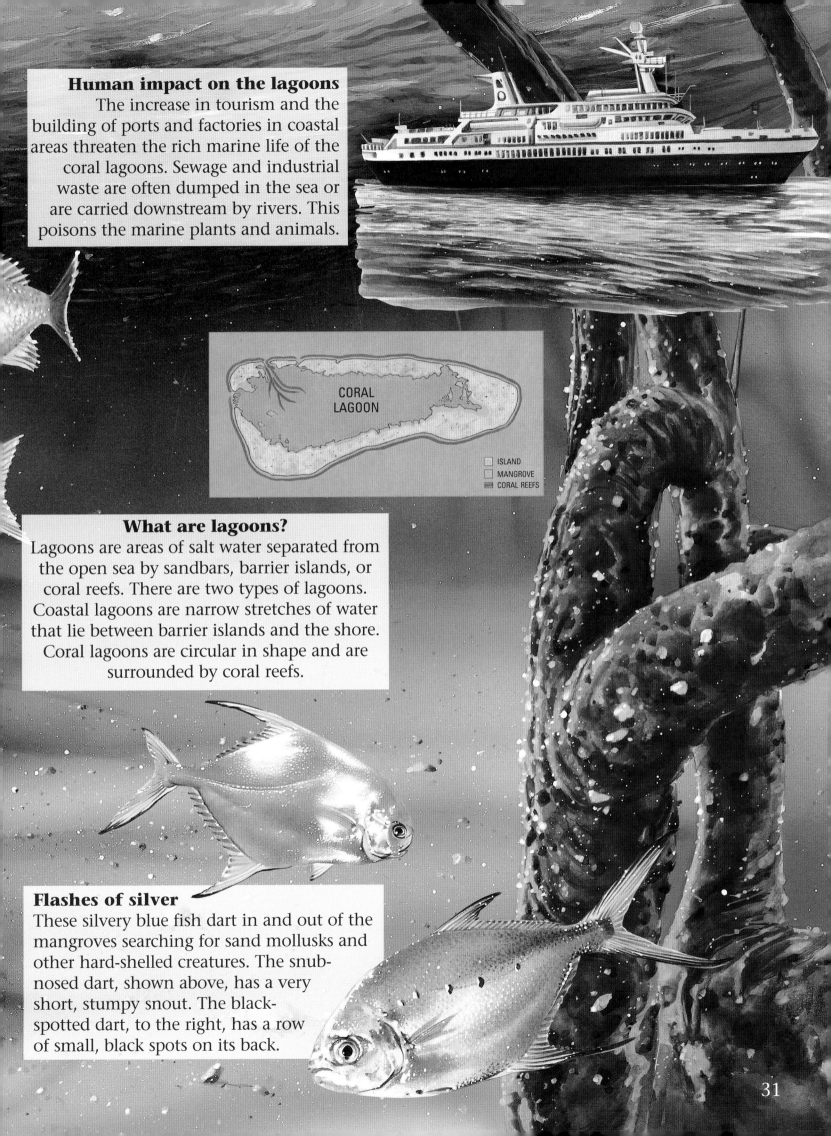

Human impact on the lagoons

The increase in tourism and the building of ports and factories in coastal areas threaten the rich marine life of the coral lagoons. Sewage and industrial waste are often dumped in the sea or are carried downstream by rivers. This poisons the marine plants and animals.

CORAL
LAGOON

ISLAND
MANGROVE
CORAL REEFS

What are lagoons?

Lagoons are areas of salt water separated from the open sea by sandbars, barrier islands, or coral reefs. There are two types of lagoons. Coastal lagoons are narrow stretches of water that lie between barrier islands and the shore. Coral lagoons are circular in shape and are surrounded by coral reefs.

Flashes of silver

These silvery blue fish dart in and out of the mangroves searching for sand mollusks and other hard-shelled creatures. The snub-nosed dart, shown above, has a very short, stumpy snout. The black-spotted dart, to the right, has a row of small, black spots on its back.

31

Coral reefs in danger

All over the world, coral reefs are under threat by coral and shell collectors, divers, and companies drilling for oil. They are also poisoned by pollution and smothered by silt and soil washed into the sea. The habitat of the reef is fragile and finely balanced. Each animal has its own special places where it feeds and lives. If one part of the reef is destroyed, the damage to the reef structure and to the food chain is quick to spread.

Shell collecting

Each year, shell collectors remove thousands of shells from coral reefs. Apart from affecting the reef's food chain, this also allows starfish, on which the shellfish feed, to increase in number and destroy large stretches of coral.

The pipe fish below is one of the many species in danger.

Oil spills

If an oil tanker runs aground, it can devastate a coral reef. Oil pours into the sea, poisoning the water and killing wildlife. Reefs are also blasted with explosives in the search for oil and other minerals.

Fishing danger

Millions of people living near the coast rely on reef fish for food and for making a living. But fishing boats can smash the coral, and overfishing puts creatures, such as sea horses, in danger of extinction.

Marine parks

Left well alone, coral reefs can recover, but it takes many years. Some countries are turning their reefs into parks to protect them. The Barrier Reef Marine Park was set up in 1975. It has special zones set aside for scientific research, fishing, and tourism.

Protecting coral reefs

Conservation groups around the world, such as Greenpeace, are working hard to save coral reefs. During the International Year of the Reef in 1997, people were able to adopt their own chunk of a coral reef.

The whale

Overfishing in the coastal reefs reduces the whale's food supply. Whales also suffer from the increase in water pollution so their numbers are decreasing. Although they are a protected species, many whales are still killed for their blubber.

Turning white

Coral is extremely sensitive to changes in the sea water. A rise in sea temperature can cause huge stretches of coral to turn white and die. This is called "bleaching." This whole coral colony (left) has died.

Fish nurseries

Mangrove swamps are valuable nurseries for fish, shrimp, and shellfish. But this precious resource is being destroyed as mangrove swamps are being drained, drowned, or smothered by the silt washed into rivers.

THE CORAL REEF GAME

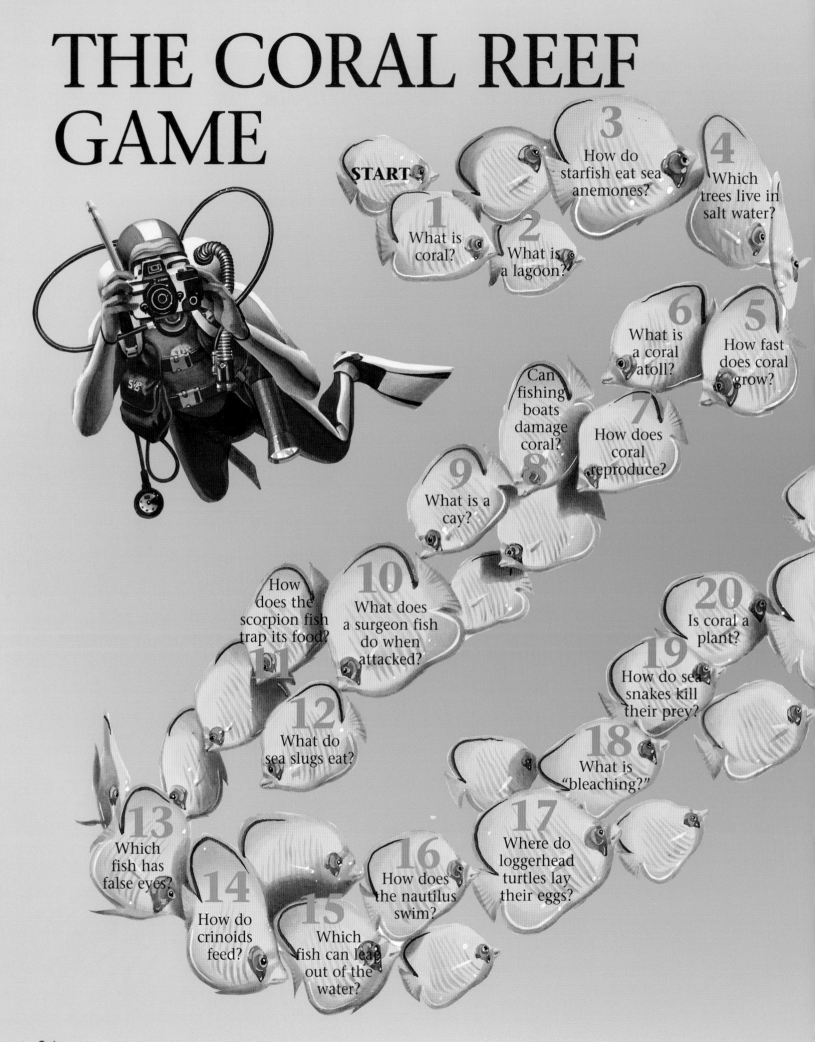

START

1 What is coral?

2 What is a lagoon?

3 How do starfish eat sea anemones?

4 Which trees live in salt water?

5 How fast does coral grow?

6 What is a coral atoll?

7 How does coral reproduce?

8 Can fishing boats damage coral?

9 What is a cay?

10 What does a surgeon fish do when attacked?

11 How does the scorpion fish trap its food?

12 What do sea slugs eat?

13 Which fish has false eyes?

14 How do crinoids feed?

15 Which fish can leap out of the water?

16 How does the nautilus swim?

17 Where do loggerhead turtles lay their eggs?

18 What is "bleaching?"

19 How do sea snakes kill their prey?

20 Is coral a plant?

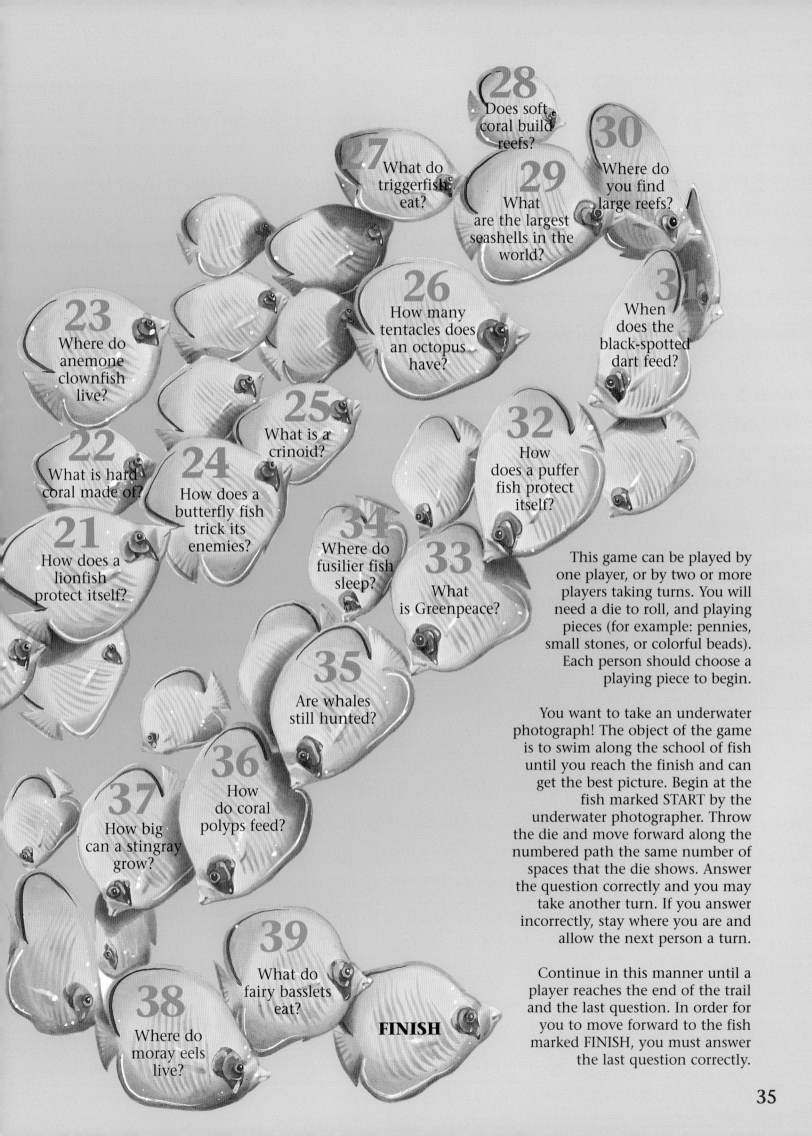

28 Does soft coral build reefs?

27 What do triggerfish eat?

29 What are the largest seashells in the world?

30 Where do you find large reefs?

23 Where do anemone clownfish live?

26 How many tentacles does an octopus have?

31 When does the black-spotted dart feed?

22 What is hard coral made of?

25 What is a crinoid?

24 How does a butterfly fish trick its enemies?

32 How does a puffer fish protect itself?

21 How does a lionfish protect itself?

34 Where do fusilier fish sleep?

33 What is Greenpeace?

35 Are whales still hunted?

This game can be played by one player, or by two or more players taking turns. You will need a die to roll, and playing pieces (for example: pennies, small stones, or colorful beads). Each person should choose a playing piece to begin.

36 How do coral polyps feed?

You want to take an underwater photograph! The object of the game is to swim along the school of fish until you reach the finish and can get the best picture. Begin at the fish marked START by the underwater photographer. Throw the die and move forward along the numbered path the same number of spaces that the die shows. Answer the question correctly and you may take another turn. If you answer incorrectly, stay where you are and allow the next person a turn.

37 How big can a stingray grow?

39 What do fairy basslets eat?

38 Where do moray eels live?

FINISH

Continue in this manner until a player reaches the end of the trail and the last question. In order for you to move forward to the fish marked FINISH, you must answer the last question correctly.

Answers to the game

1. Coral is the hard, outer skeleton of a coral polyp.

2. A lagoon is an area of saltwater separated from the open sea by sandbars, barrier islands, or coral reefs.

3. A starfish squeezes its stomach out of its body and smothers the sea anemone with it.

4. Mangroves live in saltwater.

5. Coral grows only a couple of inches (5 cm) a year.

6. A coral atoll is a round reef formed when a volcanic island sinks into the sea.

7. Some coral reproduces by forming buds and other kinds of coral release eggs into the water.

8. Yes. Fishing boats can damage coral.

9. A cay is a small coral island.

10. A surgeon fish sticks its spines upright and swipes its tail from side to side when attacked.

11. The scorpion fish traps its food by disguising itself as a rock, opening its mouth, and waiting for its prey to walk right in.

12. Some sea slugs feed on coral. Others eat sponges, sea squirts, and sea anemones.

13. The butterfly fish has false eyes.

14. Crinoids anchor themselves to a rock and fan out their feathery arms to strain plankton from the water.

15. Flying gurnards can leap out of the water.

16. By regulating the amount of gas and fluid it has inside, the nautilus can make itself float, sink, or swim.

17. Loggerhead turtles lay their eggs on the sandy beaches of a coral island.

18. "Bleaching" is the name given to coral when it turns white and dies.

19. Sea snakes use poison to kill their prey.

20. No. Coral is actually a small animal called a polyp, and is related to jellyfish and sea anemones.

21. The lionfish's feathery fins are covered in poisonous spines that it jabs at its enemies.

22. Hard coral is made of limestone.

23. Anemone clownfish live among the tentacles of the sea anemone.

24. A butterfly fish has false eye spots near its tail that trick its enemies into attacking the wrong end of its body.

25. A crinoid is a strange-looking animal with delicate feathers and brilliant colors.

26. An octopus has eight tentacles.

27. Triggerfish feed on sea urchins and crown-of-thorns starfish.

28. No. Soft coral is not a reef-builder.

29. Giant clams are the largest seashells in the world.

30. Large reefs are found in the Pacific, Indian, and west Atlantic Oceans.

31. The black-spotted dart feeds mainly at night.

32. Puffer fish inflate themselves with air or water to protect themselves.

33. Fusilier fish sleep on the sea bed.

34. Greenpeace is a conservation group.

35. Yes. Whales are still hunted.

36. Coral polyps feed by using their stinging tentacles to catch passing water creatures.

37. Stingrays can grow to more than 3 feet (about 1 m) wide.

38. Moray eels live in crevices in the reef.

39. Fairy basslets eat plankton.

Glossary

budding: one of the ways that coral reproduces. A coral polyp forms as a bud on an existing polyp.

cay: a small coral island.

camouflage: the colors and patterns on something that match or blend in with its surroundings.

cell: the smallest part of an organism.

coral: the hard, outer skeleton of coral polyps. It takes millions of polyps to form a coral reef.

crustaceans: animals, like crabs, that have segmented bodies, a shell, and pincers, and usually live in water.

discard: to throw away.

diurnal animals: animals that are active by day and sleep at night, like the lion.

echinoderms: a group of animals that often have spiny skin, such as the starfish and sea urchin.

extinction: when all the plants or animals of one species die out.

gastropods: invertebrates that usually have one foot for crawling, a head with eyes and tentacles, and sometimes a shell. Snails and slugs are gastropods.

graze: to feed.

habitats: the place where a plant or animal naturally lives and grows.

inhabit: to live.

invertebrates: animals without backbones.

lagoon: an area of salt water separated from the sea by a barrier.

nocturnal animals: creatures that are active by night and sleep in the day, like the scorpion fish.

mollusks: animals that have soft bodies and usually hard outer shells, like snails and limpets.

parasites: plants or animals that live in or on others and feed off them.

particle: a very tiny part of a substance.

plankton: tiny organisms that provide a rich source of food for fish, coral, and other sea creatures..

polyps: tiny sea animals, whose outer skeletons build up a coral reef.

photosynthesis: the process in which green plants use the energy from sunlight to make their food.

predator: animals, like the crocodile, that kill other animals for food.

prey: animals that are hunted and eaten by other animals.

sea anemone: a large polyp with petal-like tentacles around its mouth.

skeleton: the external or internal structure of plants and animals that holds them together.

species: groups of plants or animals that have the same features and that can reproduce within their groups.

tentacles: long, thin arms of animals used for feeling, moving, and for catching food.

Index